118425
Post-War United States (1945-
Early 1970s)
Marty Gitlin
AR B.L.: 7.7
Points: 2.0

Post-War United States

(1945-Early 1970s)

★★ PRESIDENTS OF THE UNITED STATES ★★

By Marty Gitlin

WEIGL PUBLISHERS INC.

Published by Weigl Publishers Inc.
350 5th Avenue, Suite 3304 PMB 6G
New York, NY 10118-0069
Website: www.weigl.com

Library of Congress Cataloging-in-Publication Data

Gitlin, Marty.
  Postwar United States / Marty Gitlin.
      p. cm. -- (Presidents of the United States)
  Includes index.
  ISBN 978-1-59036-751-3 (hard cover : alk. paper) -- ISBN 978-1-59036-752-0 (soft cover : alk. paper)
  1. Presidents--United States--Biography--Juvenile literature. 2. Presidents--United States--History--20th century--Juvenile literature. 3. United States--History--1945---Juvenile literature. 4. United States--Politics and government--1945-1989--Juvenile literature. I. Title.
  E176.1.G58 2008
  973.92092'2--dc22
  [B]

                                        2007012649

Printed in the United States of America
1 2 3 4 5 6 7 8 9 0 11 10 09 08 07

Project Coordinator
Heather C. Hudak

Design
Terry Paulhus

Photo Credits: Federal Highway Administration: page 23 (map); **LBJ Library:** pages 34, 35.

Every reasonable effort has been made to trace ownership and to obtain permission to reprint copyright material. The publishers would be pleased to have any errors or omissions brought to their attention so that they may
be corrected in subsequent printings.

All of the Internet URLs given in the book were valid at the time of publication. However, due to the dynamic nature of the Internet, some addresses may have changed, or sites may have ceased to exist since publication. While the author and publisher regret any inconvenience this may cause readers, no responsibility for any such changes can be accepted by either the author or the publisher.

Contents

United States Presidents

REVOLUTION AND THE NEW NATION (1750–EARLY 1800s)

 George Washington
(1789–1797)

 John Adams
(1797–1801)

 Thomas Jefferson
(1801–1809)

 James Madison
(1809–1817)

 James Monroe
(1817–1825)

EXPANSION AND REFORM (EARLY 1800s–1861)

 John Quincy Adams
(1825–1829)

 Andrew Jackson
(1829–1837)

 Martin Van Buren
(1837–1841)

 William Henry Harrison
(1841)

 John Tyler
(1841–1845)

 James Polk
(1845–1849)

 Zachary Taylor
(1849–1850)

 Millard Fillmore
(1850–1853)

 Franklin Pierce
(1853–1857)

 James Buchanan
(1857–1861)

CIVIL WAR AND RECONSTRUCTION (1850–1877)

 Abraham Lincoln
(1861–1865)

 Andrew Johnson
(1865–1869)

 Ulysses S. Grant
(1869–1877)

DEVELOPMENT OF THE INDUSTRIAL UNITED STATES (1870–1900)

 Rutherford B. Hayes
(1877–1881)

 James Garfield
(1881)

 Chester Arthur
(1881–1885)

 Grover Cleveland
(1885–1889)
(1893–1897)

 Benjamin Harrison
(1889–1893)

 William McKinley
(1897–1901)

THE EMERGENCE OF MODERN AMERICA (1890–1930)

 Theodore Roosevelt
(1901–1909)

 William H. Taft
(1909–1913)

 Woodrow Wilson
(1913–1921)

 Warren Harding
(1921–1923)

 Calvin Coolidge
(1923–1929)

THE GREAT DEPRESSION AND WORLD WAR II (1929–1945)

 Herbert Hoover
(1929–1933)

 Franklin D. Roosevelt
(1933–1945)

POST-WAR UNITED STATES (1945–EARLY 1970s)

 Harry S. Truman
(1945–1953)

 Dwight Eisenhower
(1953–1961)

 John F. Kennedy
(1961–1963)

 Lyndon Johnson
(1963–1969)

CONTEMPORARY UNITED STATES (1968 TO THE PRESENT)

 Richard Nixon
(1969–1974)

 Gerald Ford
(1974–1977)

 Jimmy Carter
(1977–1981)

 Ronald Reagan
(1981–1989)

 George H. W. Bush
(1989–1993)

 William J. Clinton
(1993–2001)

 George W. Bush
(2001–)

Post-War United States

In 1956, the Supreme Court declared that separating people of European ancestry and African Americans on buses was unconstitutional. This decision ended the boycott of public buses by African Americans in Montgomery, Alabama.

On August 15, 1945, millions of Americans poured into the streets to celebrate the Japanese surrender that marked the end of World War II. The celebration could not last forever. Soon, they returned to their homes to wonder what life would be like in the post-war United States.

The soldiers who had helped win the war in Europe and Asia returned to the United States and started families. The result was the greatest baby boom in the history of the nation. In 1945, the U.S. population was about 140 million. By 1965, it had reached almost 195 million.

Even though the United States and most of Europe had fought for **democracy** and freedom, many still did not enjoy those rights back home or overseas. African American soldiers were only allowed to fight alongside other African American soldiers.

African American soldiers returned to the states only to find themselves treated poorly. In the South, they were not allowed to vote or be with people of European ancestry in public places, such as restaurants. African American children attended inferior schools. African Americans were shunned throughout the country in aspects of society, such as employment and housing.

In 1954, the U.S. **Supreme Court** ruled **segregated** schools unconstitutional. In 1955, an African American woman named Rosa Parks was arrested for refusing to give up her seat on a bus. This set off a boycott of the bus system and thrust Dr.

Martin Luther King, Jr., a civil rights activist, into the American spotlight. The Civil Rights Act and Voting Rights Act of the 1950s and 1960s legally broke down racial barriers.

Meanwhile, halfway around the world, the United States became increasingly entangled in the Vietnam War. More than 58,000 U.S. troops were killed in an attempt to prevent all of Vietnam from falling to **Communism**. Communism is a form of government where the government owns everything and distributes it between the people.

The Vietnam War was the most controversial war in U.S. history. As time progressed, violent opposition grew. By 1968, most Americans had turned against the war. His unpopular policies caused Lyndon Johnson to turn down the chance at a second full term as president.

The era began with Americans celebrating the end of a war nearly all people believed in. It ended in heated debates over a war that fewer people supported every day.

The Vietnam War grew increasingly unpopular among Americans.

Harry S. Truman's Early Years

Harry S. Truman was born on May 8, 1884, to John and Martha Truman in the tiny farming community of Lamar, Missouri. John had sought a fortune in cattle trading, but failed, which forced the family to move in with Martha's parents.

Even though his family was poor, young Harry enjoyed his youth. He played with his brother and sister while their cat and dog followed them around the farm. He often spoke of those adventurous days during his adulthood. After living with his in-laws for four years, John bought a farm in Independence, Missouri.

> **"Those were wonderful days and great adventures."**
> *Harry S. Truman, on his Missouri childhood*

As a child, Truman contracted diphtheria, a disease that affects the air passages and breathing. The disease affected his nervous system, and his arms and legs were paralyzed. For six months, Truman had to be wheeled around in a baby carriage.

At school, Truman developed a strong interest in history and the lives of world leaders. He became an avid reader. He wanted to go to college, but his father did not have enough money to send him. Truman yearned to join the military. That dream was shattered when he failed his entrance exam to West Point due to poor eyesight. A few years later, Truman joined the Missouri National Guard.

Harry S. Truman's childhood was difficult, but he was a happy boy.

In 1902, Truman moved to Kansas City to help support his family. There, he worked in the mail room of a newspaper office, as a bank clerk, and as a bookkeeper.

In 1906, Truman's father requested that he come home to work the farm. Truman left Kansas City and returned home. His father died in 1914.

For a short time, Truman owned and operated a small mine and partly owned an oil business. He had little success with either business. In 1917, the United States was drawn into World War I. Truman's National Guard unit was made into the 129th Artillery Regiment.

Truman's dreams of a military life would come true after all. He was made captain of his regiment. Truman and his men fought in France and helped the Allies win the war. He earned the admiration of the men who served under him. During his time in the military, he made friends that he would keep for the rest of his life.

He appointed some of these men as his advisors when he became president. He later credited his achievements and relationships forged during the war with his career success.

Truman fought in World War I and was made captain of his regiment.

Truman's Early Political Career

After the war, Truman returned to his farm. He married his childhood sweetheart, Bess Wallace, in 1919. Less than five years later, their only child, Mary Margaret, was born.

Truman and a friend opened a men's clothing store in Kansas City. Their first-year sales hit $70,000, but rather than save some of that money, the partners invested it back into the business. A post-war economic slump soon forced the men to close the store and sent Truman into debt.

In 1922, Truman was asked to run for a judgeship. He agreed to run and he won. Truman served as a judge until 1934, when he was elected to the U.S. Senate. Truman served 10 years in the Senate. During this time, he strongly backed president Franklin D. Roosevelt. Roosevelt's New Deal policies helped rebuild America and put millions of people back to work during the **Great Depression**. The Great Depression started in 1929 when the stock market crashed, causing many people to lose their money and their jobs. During his second term, Truman saved the country $15 billion as the chairman of a Senate committee that investigated government spending during World War II.

Truman (left) became vice president under President Franklin D. Roosevelt (right).

Truman earned the **Democratic** nomination as vice-president in 1944. Roosevelt won the election, but he suffered from ill health. On April 12, 1945, President Roosevelt passed away. Truman was sworn in as the new president.

> ## "...I felt like the moon, the stars, and all the planets had fallen on me."
> *Harry S. Truman, after the death of Franklin D. Roosevelt forced him into the presidency*

When Truman entered the presidency, World War II was almost over with Germany. The war with Japan, however, was not as close to victory. The Japanese refused to surrender. To avoid sending troops to Japan and risking more U.S. casualties, Truman dropped two atomic bombs on Japan, killing thousands of people instantly. Japan surrendered soon after, ending World War II. The dropping of the atomic bombs became one of the most controversial decisions any U.S. president has made.

World War II had shifted power to the United States and the Soviet Union, the communist nation that had defeated Germany. The Soviet Union assumed control of much of Eastern Europe, installing Communist governments. In an effort to control the spread of Communism, the president asserted what became known as the Truman Doctrine.

The doctrine stated that the United States would support democracy in Eastern Europe. In 1947, Truman gave economic aid to Turkey and Greece, which he believed were being targeted for Communist expansion. The Truman Doctrine set up foreign policy for the next 40 years, particularly in fighting against Communism in Korea in the early 1950s and Vietnam the following decade. This struggle between democracy and Communism led to the **Cold War**, a war that was fought with politics, not weapons.

Meanwhile, the National Security Act of 1947 reorganized the entire U.S. foreign policy and military structure. It established the National Security Council, which included the president, vice-president, secretary of state, secretary of defense, and officials from the Central Intelligence Agency. The National Security Council integrated different departments to advise the president on matters of national security.

DESEGREGATION OF THE MILITARY

Handed down by Harry Truman on July 26, 1948, an executive order gave all men equal opportunity in the armed services. This document ended racial **segregation** in the military. Earlier that year, Truman had sent Congress a proposal to end racial discrimination in many aspects of society, including the armed forces. The proposal angered many southern politicians. By the end of the Korean War in 1953, the military was completely integrated.

Truman's Second Term

One of the best-known images of Harry Truman shows him gleefully hoisting the Chicago Daily Tribune with the headline "DEWEY DEFEATS TRUMAN" into the air. The newspaper was premature in proclaiming him defeated by **Republican** Thomas Dewey in the 1948 presidential election. Truman won by a slight margin.

> "America was not built on fear. America was built on courage, on imagination and an unbeatable determination to do the job at hand."
>
> *Harry S. Truman*

In 1949, Communists took over China. Critics claimed that Truman was unable, or unwilling, to prevent the takeover. Truman had sent his advisors to China to assess the situation. His advisors reported that no amount of funding could stop the Communist takeover. Truman decided that funds were better spent on stopping the spread of Communism in Western Europe. Soon, Wisconsin Senator Joseph McCarthy began charging that the "loss" of China was due to Communist influences in the U.S. government. Senator McCarthy led a "witch hunt" to eliminate Communists from the United States.

In 1950, China began funding troops to aid North Korea in an attempt to convert South Korea to Communism. North Korea invaded South Korea in June 1950. By the end of that year, the United States had sent troops to South Korea. General Douglas MacArthur, a World War II hero, tested Truman's resolve by insisting that U.S. troops be used to attack parts of China. The president fired MacArthur, causing a wave of criticism that sent his approval ratings plummeting.

Puerto Rican nationalists Oscar Collazo and Griselio Torresola

The *Chicago Daily Tribune* falsely proclaimed Truman's defeat by Thomas Dewey in the 1948 presidential election.

U.S. troops were sent to South Korea to fight in the Korean War.

believed that **assassinating** Truman would allow Puerto Rico to gain its independence from the United States. On November 1, 1950, they attempted to shoot their way into Blair House, where the president was living. They killed one police officer and wounded two others, but never had a chance to kill Truman.

Truman spent little time in the White House during his second term. The building was undergoing a major renovation. The main focus of the renovation was the installation of steel beams to support the original walls.

During his second term, Truman had hoped to provide peace and steady leadership. Matters, such as Chinese influence in Korea, however, prompted military involvement overseas.

Increasing tensions during the Truman administration were caused by relationships with the Soviet Union and China. Truman will be remembered for the moderation he displayed by his firm stand in supporting South Korea and stopping MacArthur when the general looked to provoke a direct war with China.

Truman chose not to run again for the presidency, and the Democratic Party nominated Adlai Stevenson. Truman retired to his home in Independence, Missouri. He followed U.S. politics until his death on December 26, 1972.

The 22ⁿᵈ Amendment

In order to prevent presidents from staying in office too long, Congress adopted the 22nd Amendment to the Constitution, which limited the presidency to two terms. The measure was ratified by the states in 1951, but since Truman was already in office and considering a run for a third term, the amendment did not become official until 1953.

Truman believed all indications pointed to a Republican takeover in 1952. Americans were tired of the Korean War. The Communist "witch hunt" led by Senator McCarthy was distressing the nation. The Cold War involving the Soviet Union and China had created tensions throughout the world.

> **"If you can't stand the heat, get out of the kitchen."**
> *Harry S. Truman, on the pressures of being president*

Adlai Stevenson addressed the crowd at the 1952 Democratic National Convention. Stevenson gained the Democratic Party's support for the 1952 presidential election.

Both parties looked to candidates who could ease the anxiety of the American people. The Democrats nominated liberal Adlai Stevenson. The Republicans chose World War II hero Dwight "Ike" Eisenhower. Eisenhower caused a stir and gained voter support 10 days before the election by proclaiming that he would go to Korea and stop the fighting.

Stevenson purposely distanced himself from Truman during the **campaign**, but the strategy backfired. The Republicans claimed that Stevenson did not want to be associated with Truman because the Democrats had performed poorly during their previous eight years in the White House.

Eisenhower continued to attack Truman. He claimed American men were dying in Korea due to his inability to train South Korean troops to fight. He said Truman was weak because he had not prevented the Communist revolution in China.

The result was a landslide victory for Eisenhower. Stevenson won only nine southern states and was swept in the rest of the country.

Dwight Eisenhower addressed the press after winning the 1952 election.

Dwight Eisenhower's Early Years

> "I have found out in later years that we were very poor, but the glory of America is that we didn't know it then."
>
> *Dwight Eisenhower*

Dwight David Eisenhower was born in Denison, Texas, on October 14, 1890, to David and Ida Eisenhower. Dwight grew up on a farm in Abilene, Kansas. Abilene had been a frequent stop for cowboys and had earned a reputation for drunken brawls and gunfights during the western expansion just a generation earlier. In fact, the legendary Wild Bill Hickok was once hired as marshal of Abilene to bring order to the town.

The stories from this period of history fascinated young Dwight.

As a child, Dwight enjoyed hunting and playing football. He did chores such as laundry, washing dishes, and cooking.

Dwight was an average student, but he excelled in math and reading. He particularly enjoyed learning about military history. Dwight's mother, who despised war, once took books on that subject away from him. She locked them in a closet to prevent him from learning more about it.

Only a small percentage of children around the turn of the 20th century attended high school, but David and Ida made certain all seven of their sons graduated. Education was

Dwight Eisenhower (seated, right) became the 34th president of the United States.

important to the entire Eisenhower family. Dwight worked for two years in a creamery to help pay for his brother Edgar's college tuition at the University of Michigan.

Soon, it was Dwight's turn to attend college. His love of military history prompted him to apply to the Naval Academy. He was disappointed to learn that, at age 20, he was too old for that institution. Undaunted, he enrolled at the United States Military Academy at West Point.

Eisenhower was surprised by the strict discipline of military life. Not only did he find it difficult to obey orders screamed out by his superiors, he proved to be no more than average in the classroom. He excelled on the football field, but knee injuries ended any thoughts of turning that talent into a career. Eisenhower graduated in the top half of his class and prepared for a career as an officer.

> "The supreme quality of leadership is unquestionable integrity. Without it, no real success is possible, no matter whether it is on a section gang, a football field, in an army, or in an office." *Dwight Eisenhower*

Dwight Eisenhower served stateside at Camp Colt, Pennsylvania, in World War I.

Eisenhower's Military Career and Presidential Nomination

Two pursuits consumed Eisenhower during his first five years as a second lieutenant at Fort Sam Houston, Texas. His professional desire was to earn a combat assignment in France during World War I. Instead, his superiors assigned him to be a football coach and teacher. He trained recruits for overseas duty, but he was not allowed to go to war.

Eisenhower proved more successful in his personal drive, which was to marry a young woman he met at a lawn party. The woman was Mamie Doud, and the two wed in 1916. The couple overcame the death of their son, Doud Dwight, who fell victim to scarlet fever at the age of three.

The man greatly responsible for Eisenhower's success was General Fox Connor. Eisenhower served under Connor from 1922 to 1924. Eisenhower regained his passion for military history and philosophy during this time.

While most people in the United States believed that World War I would be the last major conflict ever fought, Connor warned Eisenhower that another war was on the horizon. Connor helped Eisenhower gain an appointment to the Command and General Staff School in Kansas. Eisenhower graduated first in his class in 1926.

Eisenhower became a chief military aide under Army Chief of Staff Douglas MacArthur. He moved to the Philippines with MacArthur where they helped organize and train the Philippine army. When World War II broke out in Europe

Dwight Eisenhower and Mamie Doud were married in 1916.

in 1939, Eisenhower returned to the United States. He was promoted to brigadier general. Eisenhower excelled in every task presented him and soon rose to major general.

Eisenhower was too important to remain home during World War II. He was named Commander in Chief of the Allied Forces in North Africa, which was fighting a German army that had taken over nearly all of Western Europe.

Eisenhower's planning of D-Day, the Allied invasion of Europe, proved so brilliant that he was appointed military governor of the U.S. occupied zone upon the surrender of Germany less than a year later. Eisenhower was welcomed back to the United States in November 1945 as a hero. In 1950, Eisenhower became the first supreme allied commander of a group of democratic countries called the North Atlantic Treaty Organization (NATO). In 1949, countries formed NATO as an alliance to come to the defense of its members if one or more were attacked.

Though he had never held political office, a resolution circulated to nominate Eisenhower for president. The resolution gained enough momentum that Eisenhower decided to run for president as a Republican in 1952. He earned the nomination and defeated liberal Democrat Adlai Stevenson in the election.

Eisenhower had risen from mediocre student at West Point to earn the highest office in the United States. Tensions in the southern states and tensions between the United States and the Soviet Union would test Eisenhower's presidency.

> "I like to believe that people in the long run are going to do more to promote peace than our governments. Indeed, I think that people want peace so much that one of these days governments had better get out of the way and let them have it." *Dwight Eisenhower*

Eisenhower (left) became a World War II hero.

Eisenhower's Presidency and Legacy

> "Every gun that is made, every warship launched, every rocket fired signifies, in the final sense, a theft from those who hunger and are not fed, those who are cold and not clothed."
>
> *Dwight Eisenhower*

The end of World War II had left the United States and Soviet Union as the major world powers. By the time Eisenhower assumed the presidency, those two countries, as well as China, had successfully tested atomic weapons. The United States had even used atomic weapons on Japan to end the war. Atomic weapons could kill tens of thousands of people at one time. A race to see who could build up the most powerful weapons had begun. This became known as the "arms race."

Eisenhower took a firm but moderate approach to foreign relations. He continued to send troops to Korea, but he did not want to widen the war. After the Korean War ended in a stalemate, Eisenhower fought against the spread of Communism, which was established in the Soviet Union and newly adopted in China.

Meanwhile, U.S. Senator Joseph McCarthy threatened freedom in his own country by tracking down alleged communists. McCarthy used speculation and hearsay to accuse some Americans of communist behaviors in the early 1950s. Eisenhower worked behind the scenes to stop McCarthy in 1954.

Eisenhower ran for re-election in 1956. He remained popular enough to defeat Adlai Stevenson again and settled in for his second term.

In 1957, Eisenhower's intention to prevent Communist influence in other

Senator Joseph McCarthy falsely accused government officials and other Americans of being communists in the early 1950s.

parts of the world was asserted by the Eisenhower Doctrine. This doctrine stated that any country that felt threatened by a Communist takeover would receive significant U.S. aid. Eisenhower stated that the United States would use military power if there were reasons to fear an attack to the United States or any other democratic country.

Although he may not have been able to solve the Cold War, Eisenhower was able to keep the United States out of a physical war. Eisenhower can be credited with being in charge during one of the strongest economic periods in U.S. history.

Many historians believe Eisenhower's biggest failure as president was his lack of support for equal civil rights for all Americans. Although he signed the Civil Rights Acts of 1957 and 1960 that protected African American voting rights, he did not agree with the desegregation of schools.

Eisenhower was a popular president when he left office, and he is well-respected today. Eisenhower is remembered for his military achievements, as well as for his presidency.

Eisenhower left office in early 1961. After serving as a general in wartime and as a president in both war and peace, Eisenhower was ready to retire, which he did at Gettysburg Farm, Pennsylvania. During his retirement, he golfed and painted. Eisenhower suffered a fatal heart attack and died on March 28, 1969.

Eisenhower retired to Gettysburg Farm after his two terms as president.

CIVIL RIGHTS MOVEMENT

Two events that occurred during the Eisenhower administration shaped the civil rights movement, which was a movement for equality for all races.

In 1954, the Supreme Court ruled that segregated schools were unconstitutional. When the governor of Arkansas refused to integrate schools, Eisenhower sent federal troops to Central High School in Little Rock so that African Americans could attend classes there.

In 1955, Rosa Parks, an African American woman, refused to give up her bus seat on a Montgomery, Alabama, bus. Later that year, Dr. Martin Luther King, Jr., a civil rights activist, organized a boycott of Montgomery buses.

The Interstate Highway System

As a 28-year-old lieutenant colonel, Eisenhower accompanied a convoy testing army vehicles for cross-country trips. It was 1919, and World War I had just ended. The army hoped to learn how fast its transports could travel coast-to-coast. The two-lane roads snaked around many areas of the United States. The convoy crawled at an average speed of just 6 miles an hour. The painstaking journey from Washington, D.C., to San Francisco took 62 days and left a lasting impression on Eisenhower.

Another experience 25 years later brought that memory to life. While attempting to get his armies through Europe, Eisenhower noted the narrowness and poor conditions of the roads. Meanwhile, the German armies zipped quickly to their destinations on the Autobahn, a system of efficient roadways which had been built in the 1930s.

In 1954, Congress passed the Federal Aid Highway Act, which provided $175 million to build an interstate highway system. Eisenhower wanted more. He called for a highly ambitious plan that would reduce highway accidents, cut down on traffic delays, and encourage faster truck delivery of goods. The Cold War made Eisenhower believe that the country needed a quicker and more extensive escape route from cities if they experienced a nuclear attack.

Several plans to fund the highway system with an estimated cost of $27 billion were doomed to failure, but the president refused to give up. Congress finally completed legislation to pay for Eisenhower's project through a Highway Trust Fund that would receive money from a federal gasoline tax.

Both the U.S. Senate and House of Representatives gave their final approval on June 26, 1956. Eisenhower signed the measure three days later.

> "When we get these thruways across the whole country, as we will and must, it will be possible to drive from New York to California without seeing a single thing."
>
> *John Steinbeck, author, criticizing the Interstate Highway System in his book* Travels with Charley

Eisenhower's plan for the Interstate Highway System would reduce traffic, which became a big problem in the 1950s.

The interstate highway system would prove to be one of Eisenhower's greatest legacies. The system, which finally cost $129 billion, now comprises more than 40,000 miles of roads. It was completed as a cooperative venture between the federal and state governments.

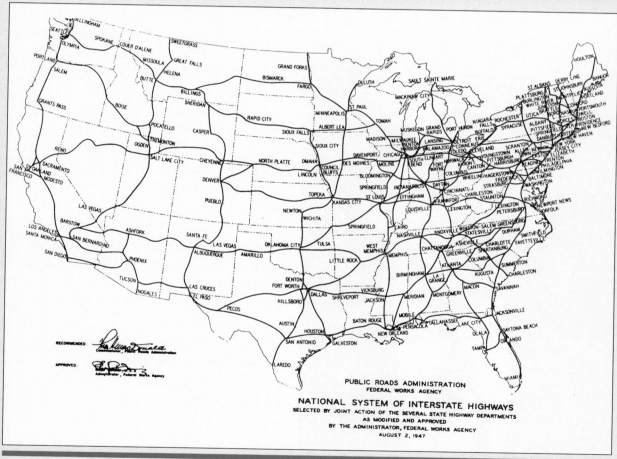

PUBLIC ROADS ADMINISTRATION
FEDERAL WORKS AGENCY

NATIONAL SYSTEM OF INTERSTATE HIGHWAYS
SELECTED BY JOINT ACTION OF THE SEVERAL STATE HIGHWAY DEPARTMENTS
AS MODIFIED AND APPROVED
BY THE ADMINISTRATOR, FEDERAL WORKS AGENCY
AUGUST 2, 1947

The original Eisenhower Interstate System laid the groundwork for improved speed and safety of travel across the United States.

John F. Kennedy's Early Years

John F. Kennedy was born to Joseph Patrick Kennedy and Rose Fitzgerald Kennedy on May 29, 1917, in Brookline, Massachusetts. The Kennedys were a wealthy, influential family. John's grandfather was active in Massachusetts politics, and his father was good friends with Franklin D. Roosevelt.

> **"Joe was the star of the family. He did everything better than the rest of us."**
> *John F. Kennedy, on his brother*

John had eight brothers and sisters. Joseph Patrick encouraged his children to strive for perfection. He demanded the best, which was easier for John's older brother Joseph Patrick, Jr., who was a brilliant student and athlete. John, on the other hand, was sickly as a child. He spent much of his youth reading in bed.

During the summers, the Kennedy family would go to their summer house in Hyannis Port, Massachusetts. The Kennedy children enjoyed swimming, sailing, and playing football.

John tried hard to live up to his father's expectations. He struggled to get good grades and played football at Choate, a prep school in Connecticut. While playing football, John suffered a back injury that he never fully recovered from. His back would bother him for the rest of his life.

In 1936, John followed his older brother, Joseph, to Harvard. Joseph had always told his family that he would become the first Catholic president, and no one doubted that he would.

John F. Kennedy, shown here at age 10, became the 35th president of the United States.

John F. Kennedy (right) and his brother, Joseph Jr. (left), visited their father, Joseph Sr. (center), in Great Britain in 1937.

In 1937, President Franklin D. Roosevelt appointed John's father as ambassador to Great Britain. John visited his father in Great Britain during the summer and took an active interest in Europe's current events.

The late 1930s were a critical time for Great Britain, which was desperate to avoid war with Germany. Great Britain set out on a policy of appeasing Nazi Germany leader Adolf Hitler, who would eventually try to take over all of Europe. Even as a college student, John was appalled when Great Britain and France agreed to allow Germany to take over part of Czechoslovakia in 1938. John feared Germany would try to take over more nations. His prophetic senior essay, *Why England Slept*, became a bestseller in 1940, just months after Germany launched World War II by invading Poland.

Kennedy's Military Career and His Rise to the Presidency

John F. Kennedy graduated from Harvard in 1940. He tried to join the army in 1941, but his bad back caused him to fail the physical exam. He exercised all summer to strengthen his back. He was able to pass the fitness test in September and was sworn in as an ensign in the navy.

Working in the Office of Navy Intelligence, Kennedy was in Washington, D.C., when the Japanese attacked Pearl Harbor on December 7, 1941. He quickly requested active duty at sea. He fought against the Japanese in the Pacific islands. Kennedy's boat was rammed by a larger Japanese ship, causing it to sink. He managed to lead his men to an island where they were rescued. His heroism earned him several medals for bravery. John's brother Joseph served in the war as a pilot. Joseph was killed in a bomber explosion in 1944.

Black smoke poured from ships on fire from the Japanese attack on Pearl Harbor.

"And so, my fellow Americans: ask not what your country can do for you—ask what you can do for your country. My fellow citizens of the world: ask not what America will do for you, but what together we can do for the freedom of man." *John F. Kennedy*

Now that his oldest son was no longer alive to fulfill his father's dreams of the presidency, Joseph, Sr., shifted his political aspirations to John. He helped John run for the Massachusetts congress in 1946. John won, and he served in the Massachusetts congress for six years.

Kennedy decided to run for the U.S. Senate in 1952 against popular Republican Henry Cabot Lodge. He and his family campaigned furiously. Kennedy's family spent $500,000 on his campaign. Most people believed Lodge would win, but Kennedy defeated him by 70,000 votes.

Soon after being elected to the U.S. Senate, Kennedy met Jacqueline Lee Bouvier, a newspaper photographer. The two were married in 1953 and had three children. The last child died as an infant.

In 1960, the Democratic Party nominated Kennedy to be their presidential candidate. Kennedy asked Lyndon Johnson to be his vice president. If not for the best-known debate in modern U.S. history, Kennedy might have lost to Richard Nixon in 1960. The first-ever televised debate, however, showed the contrast between a calm and confident Kennedy and a sweaty, nervous

THE KENNEDY FAMILY'S POLITICAL HISTORY

Many believe John F. Kennedy had a distinct advantage in his political career due to the wealth and political backgrounds of his family members. His grandfather, Patrick Joseph, the son of Irish immigrants, served three terms in the Massachusetts legislature. His father, Joseph Patrick, was the youngest bank president in the nation. He was a millionaire at age 30 and was friends with President Roosevelt. Even John's mother, Rose, had political roots. She was the daughter of long-time Boston mayor John Fitzgerald.

Nixon. Kennedy barely edged out the Republican in the November elections. At 43 years old, Kennedy would be the youngest elected U.S. president.

The Nixon-Kennedy debate was the first televised presidential debate.

Kennedy's Presidency

Kennedy was sworn in as president on January 20, 1961. One of the first things Kennedy did as president was to establish the Peace Corps. The Peace Corps is a program in which Americans can volunteer to work all over the world, helping people in other countries. Applications from young people poured in from all over the country. The Peace Corps still exists. The benefit to poorer nations and to the volunteers who participate remains one of Kennedy's positive legacies.

Just four months into his presidency, Kennedy had his first crisis. In the Eisenhower administration, the Central Intelligence Agency trained a group of Cuban exiles to overthrow the Cuban Communist leader, Fidel Castro. Kennedy went ahead with the overthrow attempt. The result was a disaster. The trained fighters were either killed or captured. The Communists not only remained in Cuba, but American relations worsened with the Soviet Union, which backed the Cuban government. This failed invasion became known as the Bay of Pigs, which is where the Cuban exile troops landed.

The Bay of Pigs invasion prompted the Soviet Union to place nuclear missiles in Cuba. In mid-October 1962, aerial photographs clearly showed their existence. The missiles had the capability of reaching most of the United States. Kennedy ordered them removed, but Soviet leader, Nikita Krushchev, refused. Some advisors told Kennedy to invade Cuba, but he opted for a naval blockade, which would prevent the Soviets from bringing any more weapons into Cuba. Kennedy demanded that the missiles already on the island be removed. Several Soviet ships were already on the way to Cuba. The world held its breath. Americans felt the country was close to a nuclear war.

Kennedy's combination of toughness and restraint prevented such a disaster. The Soviets turned back their fleet and dismantled the missile site. Kennedy was praised as a hero.

Peace Corps volunteers helped children in poor countries learn to read.

Cuban President Fidel Castro (left) had the support of the Soviet Union and its leader, Nikita Khrushchev (right).

Meanwhile, another problem was brewing half a world away in Vietnam. During the 1950s, Vietnamese Communists and nationals drove the French out of Vietnam. As the result of a treaty, Vietnam was divided into a Communist North and non-Communist South. The Viet Cong, a group of insurgents, wanted to reunite the nation under a Communist government. Kennedy sent troops to South Vietnam. He called them advisors, but they quickly became involved in combat.

At first, Kennedy was cautious to commit himself to the civil rights movement. He believed that protests would only anger people, making it more difficult to pass laws benefitting African Americans. He did, however, send federal troops to enforce desegregation in schools in Mississippi and Alabama. In 1963, a peaceful protest turned into an ugly scene in Birmingham, Alabama. Police there attacked the protesters with fire hoses, cattle prods, and police dogs. After this treatment of protesters, Kennedy decided that something needed to be done. He worked to pass a civil rights bill that eventually became the Civil Rights Act of 1964. Kennedy would not live long enough to see this act written into law.

"Our problems are man-made, therefore they may be solved by man. And man can be as big as he wants. No problem of human destiny is beyond human beings."
John F. Kennedy

Kennedy's Legacy

Although he spent less than three years as president, Kennedy will be remembered most for the new spirit he brought to the nation. He issued a challenge to the American people to promote democracy and freedom in the United States and around the world. His youthful enthusiasm and idealism had a profound effect on the country.

> "Mankind must put an end to war or war will put an end to mankind."
> *John F. Kennedy*

As president, Kennedy's positive outlook and excellent public speaking skills helped make him popular.

Kennedy feared that direct American interference in Cuba would cause the Soviet Union to invade West Germany. Many believe he should have either taken strong military action or simply left Castro alone.

Although the Bay of Pigs invasion was a disaster, it did not affect the United States as negatively as some had thought it might. Cuba has remained Communist for a half-century, and it has never posed a threat to the United States. The desire for a better life and democratic freedoms has caused many people to escape from Cuba to live in America.

Kennedy's greatest moment was not giving in to the temptation of responding militarily, yet standing firm, during the Cuban Missile Crisis. While some of Kennedy's advisors wanted to him to invade Cuba, Kennedy understood the result could have meant nuclear war. He knew he could not allow the United States to be under constant threat of destruction. His ability to size up and stare down Krushchev in such a tense time might have saved the world from a nuclear catastrophe.

Kennedy's legacy will forever be incomplete. The 1960s was dominated politically by the war in Vietnam. His future decisions regarding that war will always be cause for speculation. Though Americans began to fight and die in Vietnam under his watch, many believe he would not have escalated the conflict.

Nearly 45 years after his tragic death, Kennedy is still believed by many to be one of America's greatest presidents.

This may be because he had a vision for the nation and he expressed that vision in a way that inspired people.

On a November day in Dallas, an assassin's bullets killed Kennedy, but it could not kill that vision.

JACQUELINE BOUVIER KENNEDY

Kennedy's wife, Jacqueline Bouvier Kennedy, was a part of his presidential legacy. Jacqueline, also known as "Jackie," was a gracious, intelligent woman who captured the hearts of Americans. Jackie's first project as First Lady was to restore the White House. She set up the White House Historical Association, and she asked the country to donate furniture and art from previous presidents.

Jackie often sketched her own designs for clothing. Soon, women all over the country were copying Jackie's style. She traveled around the world, giving speeches in support of her husband.

Jackie's life may have seemed glamorous, but her family was most important to her. She was a dedicated mother to her two children, Caroline and John, Jr. When her third child, Patrick, died only days after his birth, she was devastated and mourned in private for months. Her first public trip after the death of her son was to Texas, where she would also lose her husband.

Kennedy's Assassination

Debatably, no single moment in American history has been examined in greater detail than the events that transpired in a few seconds on November 22, 1963. In a single moment, John F. Kennedy was shot while riding in an open-car motorcade in Dallas. Most Americans living at the time still remember where they were and what they were doing when they heard the news.

A 24-year-old drifter named Lee Harvey Oswald was charged with gunning down Kennedy from a nearby book depository, although Oswald never admitted to assassinating the president. Oswald was killed two days later by Dallas restaurant owner Jack Ruby in front of a stunned national television audience. With Oswald dead, the truth would never be known.

It was a sunny fall day in Dallas, Texas. Kennedy, his wife Jackie, and Texas governor John Connally waved from their limousine to cheering crowds that lined the street.

Kennedy had insisted on an open car, almost tempting fate. He preferred to wave easily and be seen by those who adored him. The crowd in Dallas appeared quite friendly, just as they were in the Texas cities of Houston, San Antonio, and Fort Worth.

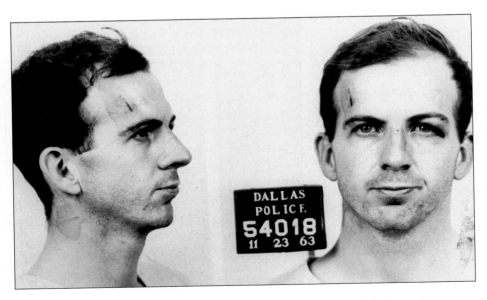

Lee Harvey Oswald posed for his police file photographs the day after Kennedy's assassination. Oswald was killed by Jack Ruby a day later.

Crowds gathered to see Kennedy on the day he was assassinated.

Shots rang out. One bullet hit Kennedy in the throat, and another entered his skull. Connally was shot in the back. After realizing that her husband had been shot, Jackie crawled to the back of the car to get help from a secret service person. Kennedy and Connally were rushed to the hospital. Doctors managed to save Connally, but Kennedy was soon pronounced dead. Jackie remained by his side, still wearing a bloodstained suit.

When Kennedy's death was announced, the nation went into mourning. A beloved president was dead at the age of 46.

Lyndon Johnson grimly took the oath of office as president.

Kennedy's body lay in state at the U.S. Capitol on November 24, 1963. The next day, more than one million mourners lined the streets as Kennedy's body was taken to St. Matthew's Cathedral. Kennedy was buried in Arlington National Cemetery. An eternal flame burns at his grave.

Kennedy's brother, Robert, campaigned for the Democratic presidential nomination in 1968. He too was assassinated.

Lyndon Johnson's Early Years

On August 27, 1908, Sam Ealy Johnson showed his newborn son, Lyndon, to a neighbor and announced that the boy would become governor of Texas one day.

Though Sam served five terms in the Texas legislature, he was not wealthy. Sam and his wife Rebekah, however, were steadfast in their desire for Lyndon to become well educated and make his mark in the world.

> **"That boy of yours…he'll never amount to anything!"**
> *Sam Ealy Johnson, speaking to his wife after a young Lyndon and his friends burned down a barn*

Lyndon was raised in what remained of the American frontier. His home had no indoor plumbing or electricity. In fact, only two homes in Johnson City had running water. Families traveled elsewhere to buy food.

Lyndon dreamed of becoming a leader. His ambitions grew after Sam returned to the Texas legislature in 1918. At age 10, he listened intently when his father's friends visited the house to discuss politics.

Lyndon's interest in politics heightened when Sam allowed him to sit in the gallery of the legislature. Lyndon would run errands for his father and fellow legislators. The highlight of his youth was accompanying Sam on the campaign trail. Lyndon stood by as his father walked door-to-door to speak with voters.

Lyndon Johnson, shown here at 18 months old, became the 36th president of the United States.

Johnson (right) was on the debate team at Southwest Texas State Teachers College.

School proved far less interesting. He received average grades, and he was often in trouble. Johnson graduated from high school at age 15. He ran away to California, where he took odd jobs before returning home. Back in Johnson City, he fell into more trouble. Johnson knew he was heading in the wrong direction. He decided to go to college and was accepted into the Southwest Texas State Teachers College.

While student teaching, Johnson developed views that would shape his philosophy as president. He taught at a school in a poor neighborhood. It struck him as unfair that some children had the advantages of wealth and others had almost nothing. Though he encouraged the kids he taught to remain ambitious, he was touched by the inequities of America.

Unless Johnson had the power to make changes, there was little he could do. Soon, that door would be open to him.

Johnson's Early Political Career

While the fortunes of most people worsened as the Great Depression gripped the United States in 1931, Lyndon Johnson's situation improved. He left his teaching position and moved to Washington, D.C. He worked as a secretary to U.S. Congressman Richard Kleberg at an annual salary that was twice what he made as a teacher.

Johnson, who worked 12 hours a day, seven days a week, was alarmed at what he considered President Herbert Hoover's lack of initiative in fighting the Great Depression. Johnson believed the government should be more active in working for a solution. The role of government in positively affecting lives became a trademark of his presidential policies.

Johnson became a huge supporter of Democrat Franklin D. Roosevelt, who succeeded Hoover. He was impressed with Roosevelt's "New Deal," which threw a large amount of government money into creating jobs and building up the country. In 1934, Johnson met Claudia Alta Taylor, who was known as "Lady Bird." The two married 10 weeks later. In 1935, Johnson was appointed as the Texas director of the National Youth Administration. This program was created by Roosevelt to provide job training for young adults. Johnson's performance earned him praise and a reputation as a tireless worker. He made the

Johnson and his wife, "Ladybird," had two daughters.

> **"We can draw lessons from the past, but we cannot live in it."**
> *Lyndon Johnson, two weeks after the assassination of John F. Kennedy*

program a huge success in Texas, enrolling 428,000 students and employing another 190,000 on work projects at the height of the depression. In 1937, Johnson ran for U.S. Congress. Johnson was an unknown, especially to voters, but a campaign strategy to link him with Roosevelt worked. He campaigned hard and earned a close victory.

Johnson lost in a bid for a Senate seat three years later, but the United States soon entered World War II. Johnson was assigned to the Navy Under Secretary's office, where he was an inspector of war progress. He served for a short time in active duty overseas.

Johnson was elected to the U.S. Senate in 1949 by a narrow margin. He moved through the ranks quickly. By 1955, Johnson was the Senate majority leader, the most powerful person in the U.S. Senate.

It took time for Johnson to establish his political image. Liberal Democrats shunned him for backing Republican president Dwight Eisenhower. He took a more liberal stand in the late 1950s with his eye on the White House. He backed civil rights legislation in 1957 and 1960 and became a vocal leader on causes relating to the struggle for racial equality.

Johnson was the U.S. Senate majority leader before becoming Kennedy's vice president.

Massachusetts Democrat John F. Kennedy won the nomination of his party for president in 1960. Believing a moderate from Texas would help him win, Kennedy named Johnson as his running mate.

Johnson never wanted to be vice president, but he accepted the job. He found that he had little power as vice president. Kennedy did not always listen to his advice, and Johnson became frustrated. Johnson did, however, take over the space program, which sent a man to the Moon in 1969. Johnson did not realize that tragedy would make him president sooner than he expected.

Johnson's Presidency

The presidency was thrust upon Johnson with the assassination of Kennedy. Johnson would not only have to soothe a grief-stricken America, but deal immediately with the many issues facing the country.

The most heated debates concerned civil rights. African Americans had stepped up their fight for equality. They were still unable to vote and attend integrated schools in the South despite laws that protected those rights. African Americans were forced to sit in a separate area in restaurants and bus terminals and were excluded from public gathering spots, such as beaches and pools.

> " ...all of us...must overcome the crippling legacy of bigotry and injustice."
> *Lyndon Johnson, urging Congress to pass the Voting Rights Act of 1965*

Johnson was sworn in as president after Kennedy's assassination. He was flanked by his wife, "Lady Bird," on his right, and Jackie Kennedy on his left.

Johnson was a firm believer in equal opportunity for all Americans. He enacted the Civil Rights Act of 1964, which banned discrimination in public places and sped up the process for school integration.

After his landslide defeat of Republican Barry Goldwater in the 1964 election, Johnson passed the Voting Rights Act of 1965, which outlawed all measures that prevented any American from exercising his or her right to vote.

By that time, however, many African Americans had become frustrated. In the next few years, African Americans would take a stand in every major city.

In 1968, Dr. Martin Luther King, Jr., the leader of the civil rights movement, was gunned down at a hotel in Memphis, Tennessee. Dr. King had advocated nonviolent protest as a means to gain equality. The nation mourned another great leader.

Soon, the nation focused on another looming problem, which was the Vietnam War. Kennedy had placed advisors there, but in 1964, it was reported that two U.S. naval ships had been attacked by torpedo boats in the Gulf of Tonkin, 11 miles off the shore of North Vietnam. Congress gave Johnson the power to take whatever measures necessary to protect U.S. interests.

Soon, Johnson ordered ground troops to Vietnam. By the time he left office in 1969, more than 500,000 American soldiers were fighting a full-scale war that eventually cost nearly 60,000 American lives and billions of dollars.

Johnson ordered an escalation of the war effort in Vietnam, including the introduction of ground troops to the battle. The war proved costly, both in terms of dollars and loss of life.

AFFIRMATIVE ACTION

The racism that had prevented African Americans from being treated fairly would not be overcome overnight. Lyndon Johnson began a policy of affirmative action, which would encourage the hiring of African Americans. Johnson believed that giving African Americans an advantage in hiring would begin to erase the disadvantage they had suffered throughout U.S. history. Affirmative action continues today.

Johnson's Great Society

Lyndon Johnson felt the American dream was something everyone should have a chance to achieve. He understood that many Americans did not have the same opportunities to share in the tremendous wealth of the nation as others did. Johnson began speaking of his goal of a "Great Society" in the United States. It would focus on government help for those in need.

The first step was the Economic Opportunity Act, which Congress passed in 1964. It was the first in a series of laws creating federal programs intended to better the lives of Americans through improved health care, education, and jobs.

Programs, such as Head Start and the Neighborhood Youth Corps, helped underprivileged children. They gave younger kids free preschool and older kids an opportunity to work. The Job Corps helped create employment opportunities. Medicare and social security allowed seniors to live fulfilling lives with fewer health concerns and less financial hardship. The Food Stamp Act of 1964 provided government money for those at the poverty level to purchase groceries.

The Great Society was a catch phrase for what Johnson envisioned for the United States. It would be a nation free of racial injustice and poverty, cities with clean air and water, schools that opened their doors to all children, and seniors who could enjoy their retirement without financial fears.

President Johnson established the Job Corps, which helped train people for jobs.

Johnson's Food Stamp Act allowed people who lived in poverty to purchase groceries.

Meanwhile, Johnson appointed African American Robert Weaver to the new cabinet post of secretary of housing and urban development. That same year, passage of the Housing and Urban Development Act gave economic breaks to tenants of new housing projects operated by non-profit organizations.

Johnson then turned his attention to education. The Elementary and Secondary Education Act gave more than one billion dollars to states to improve schools in low-income areas.

Americans embraced the Great Society ideals. Johnson overwhelmingly defeated conservative Republican Barry Goldwater in the 1964 election. However, such programs required government funding. By 1965, more of that money was going toward the growing war effort in Vietnam.

"Most of all, the Great Society is not a safe harbor, a resting place, a final objective, a finished work. It is a challenge constantly renewed, beckoning us toward a destiny where the meaning of our lives matches the marvelous products of our labor." *Lyndon Johnson*

Johnson's Legacy

Lyndon Johnson could have been remembered as one of the United States' greatest presidents, but he did not run for a second full term. His dream of a Great Society was dashed thousands of miles away in the jungles of Vietnam. Johnson's vision for the country was shattered by the loss of life and billions of dollars spent there.

The nation was losing its patience with the war, and people gathered in cities and on college campuses to protest. Johnson was hurt by chants on American college campuses such as, "LBJ, LBJ, how many kids did you kill today?"

No longer was Johnson's Vietnam policy being protested only by students threatened to be drafted to fight. Three years earlier, the war had the overwhelming support of the people, but by 1968 polls

A large crowd of students held a rally at Columbia University in New York City to oppose the Vietnam War.

Dr. Martin Luther King, Jr., was the leader of the civil rights movement of the 1950s and 1960s. He was assassinated in 1968.

showed the majority of Americans opposed the war.

With the 1968 election looming, Johnson was looking at spending months on the campaign trail while trying to run the country. With issues such as the war and increased racial tension in U.S. cities, he did not feel he could do both.

Anti-war candidates, such as Eugene McCarthy and Robert Kennedy, were gaining popularity. It was quite possible Johnson was not going to win the nomination of the Democratic Party. On March 31, 1968, Johnson announced that he would not seek another term as president.

Less than a week later, civil rights leader Dr. Martin Luther King, Jr., lost his life to an assassin's bullet in Memphis, Tennessee, causing massive riots in nearly every major American city. On June 5, Robert Kennedy was shot after speaking at the Ambassador Hotel in Los Angeles. He died the next day. Outside the Democratic convention site in late August, police clubbed and arrested hundreds of anti-war demonstrators.

The country seemed to be coming apart. No matter how idealistic Johnson's dreams and actions were, his legacy would be the Vietnam War and residing in the White House during the one of the most tumultuous periods in U.S. history.

Despite the war, this was a time of tremendous social growth in America. Johnson's war against poverty and his Great Society programs all but ended legal racial injustice. His work paved the road for more equality among the races.

Johnson's presidency was marred by the Vietnam war. Johnson's dream for America, however, should not be forgotten.

> **"I shall not seek, and I will not accept the nomination of my party for another term as your president."**
>
> *Lyndon Johnson, in his announcement to the American people in 1968*

Timeline

The changes in the United States and throughout the world were vast in the 25 years following World War II. The Cold War was not fought on battlefields, but it caused U.S. involvement in the Korean War and Vietnam War. These two wars resulted in 100,000 lost American lives, as well as heated debate and even violent protest at home.

1945-1948	1949-1952	1953-1956	1957-1960
PRESIDENTS			
Democrat Harry S. Truman becomes president in 1945 after the death of Franklin D. Roosevelt.	Truman works to battle Communist Chinese influence by sending troops to the civil war in Korea.	Dwight Eisenhower continues the war in Korea until it ends in a stalemate in 1953.	Eisenhower signs the Civil Rights Acts of 1957 and 1960 that protect African Americans' right to vote.
UNITED STATES			
Americans start families after soldiers return from World War II, setting off the largest population boom in U.S. history.	Wisconsin Senator Joseph McCarthy searches out alleged Communists in all areas of the U.S. government and society.	Americans continue to move from cities and rural areas to newly formed suburbs throughout the country.	Americans enjoy a thriving economy.
WORLD			
The United States and the Soviet Union emerge as major world powers. Europe is divided into the democratic West and Communist East.	China turns to Communism and supports North Korea in starting a civil war with South Korea in an attempt to unify the country under Communist rule.	Rebellions against the Communist governments in East Germany and Hungary are put down by the Soviet Union.	Cuba is added to the growing list of Communist countries. 

In the last 10 years of the era, the nation began living out its creed that all people are created equal. The progress made in civil rights was painstaking and often chaotic, but the work of presidents such as Eisenhower, Kennedy, and Johnson played critical roles in bringing about change. The era began with Americans proud of their efforts in World War II. Nearly everyone agreed the war was necessary. The era ended with anger and division over an increasingly unpopular conflict, the Vietnam War, half a world away.

1961-1963	1964-1965	1966-1968
PRESIDENTS		
Kennedy faces off with the Soviet Union during the Cuban Missile Crisis.	Lyndon Johnson signs the Civil Rights Act and Voting Rights Act to help ensure equal protection for African Americans, particularly in the South.	The growing unpopularity of the Vietnam War causes Johnson to reject a run for a second term in office.
UNITED STATES		
Americans mourn the assassination of President Kennedy in 1963.	African Americans in large cities take a stand for racial equality.	Civil rights leader Dr. Martin Luther King, Jr., and Democratic presidential candidate Robert Kennedy are assassinated during a two-month period in 1968.
WORLD		
The Soviet Union builds the Berlin Wall to prevent East Germans from fleeing to the West.	Increased U.S. involvement escalates the war in Vietnam.	An attempt at democratic reform in Czechoslovakia is crushed by a Soviet-led invasion.

Activity

Dr. Martin Luther King, Jr., organized peaceful protests and advocated a strategy of nonviolence in order to gain equal rights for African Americans.

Think about the world around you. What is happening in the world that you think is unfair? Why is it unfair, and who or what suffers because of this unfairness? What can you do to make this situation more fair? Have other people tried to solve this unfairness before? If so, how?

Did they use violence? How can you help without resorting to violence? How can you encourage others to peacefully stand up for their cause?

Write out the answers to these questions. Once you are done, talk to a teacher, parent, or another adult about your cause. Can they help you put your plan into action? You might just change the world like Dr. Martin Luther King, Jr.

Quiz

1. True or False? Harry Truman won the 1944 election to become president.

2. In which country did the United States fight against communism in the early 1950s?
   A. Germany
   B. Vietnam
   C. Korea

3. John F. Kennedy was assassinated in what city?
   A. Houston, Texas
   B. Los Angeles, California
   C. Dallas, Texas

4. What U.S. politician led a search for alleged Communists throughout the United States?
   A. Joseph McCarthy
   B. Adlai Stevenson
   C. Sam Rayburn

5. Dr. Martin Luther King, Jr., led an African American boycott of buses in what southern city?
   A. Atlanta, Georgia
   B. Montgomery, Alabama
   C. Miami, Florida

6. True or False? Eisenhower was a World War II hero.

7. True or False? The United States fought on the side of North Vietnam during the Vietnam War.

8. Lyndon Johnson was born and raised in what state?
   A. Texas
   B. Oklahoma
   C. Arizona

9. True or False? Johnson was defeated in his bid to be elected to a second term in office.

Answers 1. False. He took over upon Franklin D. Roosevelt's death in 1945. 2. C 3. C 4. A 5. B 6. True 7. False. The United States fought with South Vietnam against North Vietnam. 8. A 9. False. He declined to run for a second term.

Further Research

Books

To find out more about U.S. presidents, visit your local library. Most libraries have computers that connect to a database for researching information. If you enter a keyword, you will be provided with a list of books in the library that contain information on that topic. Non-fiction books are arranged numerically, using their call number. Fiction books are organized alphabetically by the author's last name.

Websites

The World Wide Web is also a good source of information. Reputable websites usually include government sites, educational sites, and online encyclopedias. Visit the following sites to learn more about U.S. presidents.

The official White House website offers a short history of the U.S. presidency, along with biographical sketches and portraits of all the presidents to date. **www.whitehouse.gov/history/presidents**

This website contains background information, election results, cabinet members, and notable events for each of the presidents. **www.ipl.org/div/potus**

Explore the lives and careers of every U.S. president on the PBS website. **www.pbs.org/wgbh/amex/presidents**

Glossary

assassinating: murdering a significant political figure

campaign: the competition by rival political candidates leading up to an election

Cold War: the tense relationship between the United States and the Soviet Union

communism: an economic and social system based on government ownership of businesses and resources

democracy: a form of government giving people basic guarantees, such as freedom of speech, freedom of the press, and freedom to protest

Democratic: one of two major political parties in the United States, generally considered more liberal

Great Depression: a period of severe economic hardship in the United States in the 1930s

Republican: one of two major political parties in the United States, generally considered more conservative

segregated: to be separated based on race, religion, or gender

Supreme Court: the highest court of law in the United States

Index